Louie Lizard and the Stowaway Adventure

C. Collier

Copyright © 2020 C. Collier

All rights reserved. No part of this book may be reproduced or transmitted in any form or by any means, electronic or mechanical, including photocopying, recording or by any information storage and retrieval system without permission in writing from the publisher.

IMAGINATIVE MIND BOOKS—Saddlebrook, NJ
ISBN: 978-0-578-80927-4
Library of Congress Control Number: 2020923762
Title: *Louie Lizard and the Stowaway Adventure*
Author: C. Collier
Digital distribution | 2020
Paperback | 2020

This is a work of fiction. The characters, names, incidents, places, and dialogue are products of the author's imagination, and are not to be construed as real.

Dedication

Dedicated to: Rose and Nick, and their home in Florida, where the Real Louie lives. And Rob for bringing me to Florida.

It was a usual warm sunny day with warm breezes in the air. Louie loved to feel the warm air over his cool skin; this was his favorite thing in his whole world

Sometimes it would get too warm and he would try to sneak into the BIG area that the people lived in and run across the floor there which had tile on it and it was cool.

Sometimes the people inside would see him and the girls of them would scream. The little boy would always try to catch him. Louie learned to check the open door first before entering so that he would not lose his freedom to come and go as he pleased. One time the little boy did catch him and put him in a box. Louie didn't like the box. It had no sunshine, no warmth and no tile in it. It was very uncomfortable.

He had managed to escape it and found the big door open. He had run as fast as he could until he reached the soft green grasses of the yard and beyond. His Momma had warned him of this hazard but Louie was always curious and loved to explore and travel. Momma had told him of others who never returned from the BIG house. No one knew what became of them. This just made Louie more curious. But as always, with curiosity can come danger. Louie learned this when the little boy caught him and since then and his escape he was more cautious when he entered the BIG house and he learned to run very fast and HIDE. Louie knew how to hide very well. There were a million places to hide in the BIG house. He just had to be careful that he had a way to get outside again.

The people did not always live in the house. There were long periods of time when they were not around and sometimes they came with other people and the house would be too full for Louie to attempt to visit the tile floor. On those days he would just lie around in the soft tall grasses and occasionally bask in the sun attached to the tall wooden posts. He had heard the people call these fences, but he did not know what they were, just that they were nice to hang on to when basking in the sun. The people would often see him there and stare. Louie would always stay very still unless they got too close, then he would almost fly and dive into the tall grasses that he could hide in out of their reach.

Life for Louie was good. He loved everything. Even the rain. In the rain he could cool off and relax and he always found a nice reed to hang on to and he was good at it. Still Louie longed for an adventure. He was still a youngster by lizard standards and adventure always calls to a youngster. Even though some adventures could be dangerous Louie still felt he was missing out on something.

One particularly warm Florida day, Louie noticed that the people had returned. He also noticed that there were only about 5 of them. Four older ones and just one boy, a little older than the other boy that usually came to visit. Louie spent what seemed like hours just watching this boy to see if it would be safe to enter the BIG house and enjoy the cool tile floor.

One day Louie noticed the big door was open and beyond laid the cool tile. He carefully looked around and noticed that the people had forgotten to close it. How silly he thought, but a bit of luck for him. He could enjoy the tile without fear of being seen and have plenty of time to then return to the tall grasses. He entered and immediately could feel the coolness on his feet. He scampered across the tile and notice there was not one of the people around at all. With a sigh of relief he stretched out fully and enjoyed it all. After a while, as it was with Louie, he got curious and set out exploring areas he had never gone before. There were very large areas and small areas and in one area in particular he found what seemed to be an open box on the floor. It was filled with soft things, things he had seen on the people. Since no one was around Louie scampered into the open box. Funny the box was also soft, not like the box the one boy had tried to keep him in No this one was soft like the items inside it. It was cool and cozy and ooh so comfortable. Louie stretched out to enjoy it.

He must have drifted off to sleep for a while when a noise of people startled him awake. Louie knew the people had returned and he had to make it to the door to the tall grasses before they closed it. It was too late. Staying hidden the whole time, Louie saw the door was closed and the people were about inside. He noticed that none of them seemed to bother with the big soft box he was in, so he returned to it and found that there were many areas inside it to hide. Nestled inside, safely, Louie knew he had to wait for them to open the big door before he could do anything. After a time the people started laying down on the big soft squares and the lights in the house went out. Louie felt safe for the night, so off to sleep he went. He figured in the daylight he would try to find a way to escape.

The morning came and with it some fear for Louie. The people had woke up and started moving about very fast. Louie never saw this before. They were laying more soft things in the soft box, right on top of where he was hiding!!! Louie hung on and stayed right where he was as he knew if he ran out now they would find him and he could only imagine the outcome of what that would mean. Before he knew it the soft box was closed up and he could not get out and then the soft box was being lifted in the air. Louie felt sick. He had never been so high up before and it made him dizzy. He figured the best thing to do was just rest until it came down again. Well it did. Many times. Up and down, down and up and back again. He had eaten before entering the big house and now it was upsetting his tummy, after what seemed like forever, it finally settled. There was a strange feeling of humming that seemed to last and last. Louie did not know how long this went on as lizards only know day and night and it all runs together.

After so so long, the up down, down up happened again only now Louie was so hungry and that didn't help his tummy either. This up down finally settled also and then the box opened. He could feel the soft things inside being moved around and touched. He knew the people were very close. He tried to hide under the items. After a time it was his tail that gave him away. The people who were in the soft box was the other boy. He caught sight of Louie's tale and Louie could hear the boy talking. It seemed he was talking to him. If only he knew how to talk back but alas he had never fully learned the language the people spoke in.

   The boy was frantically trying to coax Louie out of the soft box. Louie started to shake, he was scared and hungry and he just wanted to go back to the tall grasses and see his Momma.

With his strength failing him, he slipped and the boy finally was able to cup him in his hands. Louie was lifted so high he feared he would fall. But the boy held him gently and placed him in a clear box. In the box was grass! Water, and food! This was so not like the box the first boy had put him in. After a time, A light was also shining on him   He knew it was not his most favorite sun but it felt warm and after all he'd been through Louie welcomed the warmth of the light it was helping his tummy to settle and the food was not his usual but it was pretty good.

Louie had no idea how long he was going to live here or what would become of him but for the time being it was okay. One day the boy cupped his hands and took Louie out of the clear box and brought him to one of the look throughs in the house. Through it Louie could see white. Such a white he had never seen in all his life! What was it? The boy had some of it inside and let Louie touch it. OOOOHHHH it was SOOOO cold!
Louie had never seen anything like it, nor felt anything like it. He noticed that after a time it stopped being white and became like water, just very cold water...

Louie touched the clear look through and that was cold also. Through it he could see the outside but it was not the outside he knew. It was all white and cold and he could not see any green grasses. There were the tall wooden items, but that white stuff was on them. They did not look comfortable. Soon after, the boy gently put Louie back in the clear box and it was warm again.

Sometimes the boy was gone for a long long time. But he always came back and always would talk to Louie. Louie did not understand him but he would listen anyway. Somehow he knew this boy would not hurt him. Life went on like this for Louie for some time. Over the long long times the boy was gone, Louie wondered if he would ever see his beloved grasses and sun again and of course his Momma. This made him sad, but after all he wanted an adventure. He had no idea where he was and he was sure that his Momma was probably worried and feared the worst for him. He was sure that his fellow lizards figured he was gone like the others in the past.

He wondered if this is where the others who had never returned ended up. He did not see any of them where he was now, but wondered if there were other places like he was in now and if that is where they were. Even though he did not understand what the boy and the big people said he could feel some of what they were saying by the way they touched him.

Life for Louie would be okay he thought, but oh how he missed his home and the warmth of the real sun.

One day, the boy cupped his hands and took Louie to the big soft square that the people laid down on at the time of no sun. It was soft. And large, especially to Louie. He was afraid to move. The boy was next to him talking and even though he could not understand he felt the boy was sad too. He held something to Louie and he thought he saw another lizard!!!!!! It took sometime but Louie realized it was not another lizard. So this is what I look like he thought. Wow. Louie always figured he was brown, but now he looked so pale. Was this what was making the boy sad? He and the boy stayed there for a while.

One thing Louie knew was that he was always tired here. Soon the boy put him back in the clear box and he felt a little warmer and he wondered if his nice brown color had returned. The boy put the something in the clear box with Louie and now Louie could see himself all the time whenever he wanted.

It did not seem that his nice brown color was going to return. Even if this was or was not the reason the boy was sad, Louie was sad. He missed his nice warm brown color. After all it was who he was.

One day, the boy came and put a lid on the clear box. Then the box started to move. Louie hung on. What was happening?? The box was in the air. That same up down feeling he had so very long ago. Through the clear box Louie could see around him. He was up high and moving. He was not falling, but moving. The box was being placed into another box, an even bigger one. That box was closed and then that box was moving. He also noticed the soft box with the soft items in it was also inside this new big box that was moving also. All this moving and not on your own feet. The dizziness was returning. Louie somehow knew the boy would keep him safe so he slept. He needed to sleep. He was so weak lately.

When he woke up, he was so hungry. But in his clear box was food. So he ate something, but slowly. He remembered how his tummy felt the last time and he did not want that again.

This seemed to go on for quite some time. Louie wondered if this was going to be his life now. He hoped not. He liked the clear box when it was still and not moving so much better.

Soon the big box that they were all in stopped moving and the soft box was taken out and then his clear box was also taken out. He could see that he was up high again and that he was moving. It was another BIG house!!! It had been such a long long time, but Louie was pretty sure he recognized this BIG house. It was dark so it was night this he knew and the boy placed the clear box in the big house. After a time, Louie slept and then he awoke to warmth. Such brightness. The boy had come and removed the lid to the clear box and again gently cupped his hands and lifted Louie out. He placed Louie on a familiar surface. THE COOL TILE FLOOR!!!! Louie never thought he'd ever see that again, but he recognized it!!! He was a bit weak but his feet still moved although not as fast as he could remember. But he did remember the big door and he saw it. Carefully the boy followed him as he scampered slowly across the tile floor to it.

Just beyond the door Louie could see TALL GRASSES. Were these HIS tall grasses that he remembered and loved so well? He could see the tall wooden things! And once he reached the door he could feel that familiar warmth!!! Yes it was his sun!! Oh it was so warm!!! The warmth felt so so good to Louie. The boy followed Louie carefully and watched his every move. Once outside the big door, the boy placed some food and water on the edge of the big solid slab that Louie used to bask on. He was hungry. Would he remember how to find the food again on his own? It had been so long since he had to do that for himself.

This would happen for a little while each day the sun would rise. The boy would follow him outside and put food out for him and stay with him. Eventually Louie started to feel strong again and once in the look through he caught a glimpse of what he now knew to be himself and he could see he was that nice warm brown color again!!!! This made Louie very happy. He wondered if his Momma would ever remember him if he could find her. One day, the boy did not follow Louie and he was left on his own. So he wondered through the tall grasses and basked in the sun and found that he could still climb the tall wooden things. Then it rained and he hoped he'd be able to hang on to the wooden things and he was surprised he could still do it. It had been so so long he felt since he had been able to do that.

The next day that wonderful warm sun was shining brightly and Louie was enjoying basking in it when he heard something in the tall grasses. A voice he recognized poked through the grasses. He understood it. He had not understood any voices in so long. But this voice knew him and who he was!!! Yes, it was Momma and other lizards. They were so surprised to see him!! Louie, momma said, you were gone so so long we feared we'd never see you again. Where have you been? He ran to her and was so so happy to see her. Momma, I have so much to tell you!!! Momma said well, it seems to me you finally had your adventure!! Yes momma I did. I must tell you all about it and the up and down and down and up and the clear box, the soft box, the other food, the white cold and clear look through. I never thought I'd see you or anyone I knew again.

And that is how it went for Louie. The other lizards would always seek him out and listen to his tale of his adventure. Louie never returned to the big door or the tile floor after that he had had his adventure and he was content. But every once on a while he would catch one of the people looking at him basking on the tall wooden thing and he knew it was the boy. He remembered him and he was thankful that the boy took good care of him and provided him with his adventure of a life time. Yes, Louie had the life he always wanted and was finally happy.

The End.

About the Author.

C. Collier, lives in New Jersey but travels frequently to Pennsylvania and Florida. Good stories come from good travel and an inventive mind, like that of a child.